Dancing in Santa Fe

and other poems

Beate Sigriddaughter

Červená Barva Press
Somerville, Massachusetts

Červená Barva Press
P.O. Box 440357
W. Somerville, MA 02144-3222

www.cervenabarvapress.com

Bookstore: www.thelostbookshelf.com

Cover: Images courtesy of Hubble.org and Wikimedia Commons

Cover Design: William J. Kelle

ISBN: 978-1-950063-23-9

Praise for *Dancing in Santa Fe and other poems*

Beate Sigriddaughter's *Dancing in Santa Fe and other poems* will make you remember what it is to be alive in this world. Insightful, rewarding poetry. These poems moved me. They are filled with heart and care and apology and exquisite writing. They explore the darkness as well as the awesome beauty of life, and how, as human beings with a soul and memory, we must learn to live with both. These poems question and consider, looking inward as well as to the physical world, and to the mystical and spiritual. Ultimately, they lift a dark curtain, and are laced with love.
—Kari Nguyen, Contributing author, *The Best of Boston Literary Magazine* **(***Volume One***) and** *New Hampshire's Emerging Writers Anthology* **(2018)**

Were I forced at the point of King Arthur's sword to sum up Beate Sigriddaughter's poetic voice in three words—not counting the audible *gulp* at such a daunting demand—my response would be a strong, defiant, "Redolent of Life!" (The exclamation point my proud, subversive fourth.)
—Mathew Paust, author of *Executive Pink,* **whose blog** *Crime Time* **is at https://mdpaust.blogspot.com**

ACKNOWLEDGMENTS

Many thanks to the editors of the literary magazines in which the following poems first appeared, some in slightly different form:

Cultural Weekly: "Dancing in Santa Fe"
Dissident Voice: "Lines for a Princess"
The Linnet's Wings: "The River," "Wanderer's Night Notes"
Mojave River Review: "The Bible"
The Peregrine Muse: "Samsara," "Nirvana," "Scheherazade"
Salome: "The Seven Ravens: Notes on the Fairy Tale"
Silver City Quarterly Review: "Joy"
Tuck Magazine: "Silence"
The Write Place at the Write Time: "Rules for the Road," "The Most Beautiful Music," "The Dragon's Tale"

TABLE OF CONTENTS

Acknowledments

About the Author

Dancing in Santa Fe

and other poems

The Seven Ravens:
Notes on the Fairytale

Once upon a time
a princess found her brothers
had been turned into ravens because
her father, the king, wanted a girl
and at her Christening one of the boys
made a mistake. So the king cursed
them all to live as ravens evermore.

Of course once she found out,
the girl immediately set out
to save them. The journey took her
as far as the sun and the moon
and some especially helpful stars.
She cut off her little finger when
she noticed she had lost the key
to the glass mountain door
where her raven brothers lived
under the glass ceiling.
Her little finger did the trick,
unlocked the mountain, reunited
her with her brothers and unraveled
the careless curse.

Interesting, though, if seven girls
were cursed because of one son,
it wouldn't even be noticed.
It happens all the time.

Dancing in Santa Fe

I.

How beautiful you are,
world, with jewels in the juniper
moments after rain. When
will I be allowed to touch
your beauty and keep it
alive?

II.

As soon as I encountered history
and Hitler, I became the enemy.

This is not a fairy tale
where a curse can be undone
by climbing glass mountains
or making sudden sacrifice.

III.

I came to dance late
and at my age it isn't easy
to find a partner. So when Chico
and I jelled in Santa Fe
at the Skylight and danced
better than I had danced in years
and danced past midnight
and found it difficult to leave,
of course I agreed to meet again
with his friends at Tiny's Restaurant
and Lounge my last night in town.

IV.

Gabriel danced okay, but he was born
in Hamburg. The band went on
break. We had a country in common,

though he went to America
as a wee babe. He had just come back
from Germany to visit roots, including
Bergen-Belsen concentration camp
where much of his family had perished.
Gabriel, all I could ever do is honor
your pain.

V.

I kept wanting to say,
as I have wanted to say
so many times in my long life,
"I wasn't even born yet."

And as so many times before
I kept my irrelevant silence.

VI.

I also wanted to say, "I only
came to dance." Same silence.

Meanwhile, Marcus
at our table found my discomfort so
exquisite, he wanted to continue this
most captivating conversation
at lunch someday, or, since
it turned out to be my last night
here in Santa Fe, then maybe coffee,
now. I declined and soon left.

VII.

For days I was flooded
off and on with tears. Not a lot
of comfort at home, just
helpless witnessing. Who,
not born German, can possibly
comprehend the guilt I am condemned

to feel for sins I haven't committed?
It is an unspeakable filter
on this gorgeous world.

I haven't danced much since.

VIII.

The war has been over
for more than seventy years.

The war is never over.

I grew up asking, "May I
go play in the ruins?" Mostly
the answer was yes. Once
in a while a child found a bomb
and we were grounded
for a few days or weeks.

IX.

I don't want to live with this
guilt like a lead shield
that shelters my heart
and lungs from dangerous rays.

I wasn't—the war—born yet
is never over.

X.

A favorite heirloom: a browning
piece of paper, January 16, 1948—
I wasn't born yet—declares
my father "nicht betroffen,"
not incriminated.

XI.

I live a dream. Earth under my feet,
birds loud at the window, deer stroll
by, lizards dash on the wall, a husband
in my arms at night, rivers not too far
away, snakes, roses by the kitchen
door from April to early June, and again
from August to November, though
lilacs bloom only once, a juniper
that might be older than I am.
But no wise creature here to tell me
what task to undertake to undo
the curse that keeps me uneasy
in this shimmering world. Only
the wind in the juniper sings this
is the task that has been given
to you. Sometimes I feel I am blind.

XII.

I want to honor you, life,
by living with joy. The enemy
within just laughs. Those others,
they just wanted to live, never mind joy.
Your sister, dead in 1945. The Jews
in concentration camps. The children
who played too close to bombs.
Their chances gone forever.
The enemy within is strong.

XIII.

Once you learn to dance
you never forget.

Samsara

samsara, literally: passing through

I am a wanderer in love.
Ten thousand things and more
at my feet. Perhaps
I am the tarot deck fool imagining
the precipice is just not relevant.

In the east the sun. I love
beginnings, the open sudden
cliffs, look, a monastery, and
beyond the juniper the town, below
slick rock ready for lizards
and the occasional snake.

From up above the town looks
safe, its circus of distance still
humming of a long-haired prince,
a silk rope in one hand, a girl
in the other. I would love to be
part of all that flying, a trapeze
of trembling certainty.

The mountain path is safer,
with no responsibility beyond
adoring the untrammeled four
white petals of a fendlerbush,
or at night Orion, easy
to find, soon sinking away
for summer. He will be present
still, but invisible, as so much
of great importance often is.

Even on the mountain, surrounded
by excellence, the trouble
of the city clamors in my heart
while blossoms recede and lizards
zip out of the way into comfort
with swift splendor. Under the radar

the original question, quite childish,
remains: Why

is there war? This world, with so much
beauty. Why all this
dishonor, a dreadful burden
handed down
from one generation to the next?

I spread my arms with hope as flowers
reappear, steep with attention and cliffs
at my feet. This life a sacred loan.
I vow to celebrate.

Nirvana

nirvana, literally: blown out, extinguished

No, I don't trust this. I never have.
Yes, yes, of course I crave
enlightenment like everybody else.

On the top of the mountain an angel
(or a lizard, or a ladybug) explains:
Nirvana means a withering of all,
especially those pesky desires, until
none are left, no yearning, no hunger, no
anxiety, no greed, no wild love,
just self-effacing consent.

And isn't that like suicide?
I ask, in order to avoid the pain
of dying, the inevitable loss
of life? I still want to celebrate
this charm of samsara,
where animals and trees do what needs
to be done, where in the circus of cities
we conduct our sweet and bizarre
rituals of hunger and yearning.

But long before I can articulate,
the angel or lizard or ladybug leaves.

I love you, world. Send more angels.
Help me fight the dull and dangerous
deceptions. Let me not renounce
the hungry finches, the wandering
friends, your juniper green,
the trembling fever of the wind.

The River

Its strength declares wild green
indomitable presence, even across
the desert. It carves canyons, casts
capricious waterfalls with or without
applause, it plays music you cannot
predict any more than you could
predict the jostle of a fine kaleidoscope.
It listens in the sun and whispers
eerie melodies of comfort and eternity.

I want to sing to it: flow, river, flow,
until I understand the magic
of indifference, the sultry patience,
dancing like a pilgrim among junipers
and lilacs, alone by the blue thread
of water, instead of stumbling
in the wind of yesterday.

I am not a river, I am bound
to longing and dissatisfaction,
and today I love all that. Let me carve
crevices and canyons, passageways
through mountains of unnecessary evil.

Wanderer's Night Notes

Tonight I am tired. This valley
of tears and of fears, this footpath
of grief where you walk
barefoot among scorpions, closing
your eyes, convincing yourself
it doesn't matter, all is well.
It isn't. We aren't.

I pray for courage to dance
my anger now, my fear, my dreams,
and dance my hunger loudly. This
is not how it was supposed to be.
What is the point of limping through
this superfluous life? Why
not make it a pleasure for each other
instead of this torment of acceptance
of puny bits of nothing much?
Life, make it for my anger
to not be necessary. Make beauty
fall like morning dew, and sadness
burn away debris with fire. Let me love
with pure gold and grandeur.

                                 Teach me
your scratchy ropes. I will learn.
I will climb. I will love.

Rules for the Road

High on the mountain things are carved
solidly into the tender granite of your soul:

Life is a gift, not a duty. Honor it.
And celebrate.

Honor yourself,
your tenderness, your loud exuberance.

Honor your spirit of passion.

Honor your ancestors.

Honor your children.
This one is very important.

Honor love.

Honor the rocks you walk on and the trees
who give you breath.

Honor your hunger, your desire.

Honor the ravens and the flies.

Honor the fears that meet you
in the middle of the night.

Stop war.

Honor beauty.

Live deeply.

The Most Beautiful Music

November 2016

Now I have time only for the most beautiful music.
— Jónas Ingimundarson, pianist, cancer survivor

My world is not well. I seem to wander
in the midst of a great cancer of the soul.
Trinkets have multiplied and grown
out of control. This fear in my bowels
I have never felt before. I try to learn
from others, as I stumble on. My gentle
neighbor, eighty-three, Hispanic, walks
with a limp. He is afraid. He mentions
praying often. He suspects that God
is punishing us and we don't even know
what sins we have committed. Up
on the ridge of the mountain I sometimes
meet a woman who spends hours each day
sitting with the sun and the rocks, summer
or winter, sending healing energy out
into the world. Grandfather Golden Eagle
tells me to bless the world with my eyes
each time I look at anything. Make every
sight count. I try. I am afraid. A friend
posts on Facebook, three lines of gratitude
each day to counteract the terror in our bones.
Earth is our bones. The sun. I listen
to Mariachi bands, church choirs, poets—
oh, the poets, so diligent in coming across
with blessing and caressing this world.

We are not here to be overtaken by trinkets.
We are here for the song of the sun, the light
of many-throated birds, and Mariachi bands
with golden sombreros, the decency
of offering each other beauty and joy, the pleasure
of being alive at sunrise, and at sunset still.

We are the voice of God. Let us fill
the narrow margins of reality with beauty.

Scheherazade

How I wanted to play
with your beauty, study breathlessly
at your feet, drink your wise stories,
touch the bursting jewels in your dress,
blue silk with threads of green and gold
to lace the magic in place. Your name
is a braid of freedom, spirit, survival,
flawless peacock feather dreams,
mother of pearl, all shiny. Your courage,
your knowledge, one thousand books
by heart, ten thousand thoughts
while conjuring up stories to save
your life and others after you.

I have heard
how not forgiving is like drinking
poison, hoping the unforgiven will
suffer. This always rattles me. I cannot
forget the bloodshed that preceded you,
one virgin used per night. The graves,
where did he discard the bodies?
I cannot forget this, not even
wandering alone in moonlit mountains,
listening to a thousand and one voices
of the night wind as it weaves
above your pleasantries.

Perhaps after a while you no longer
notice. After all you are one in a million,
the one held up to all of us—if we
were only smart and sexy like that,
spreading our legs on exotic sheets,
or standing by some strident microphone
for some man's pleasure, lights flashing,
all manner of music playing to advantage,
using a most operatic voice.

I bless your incense in farewell, your
bright innocence, your gullible glory,
your amazing perfume, branded with
absolution, impressing the enemy until
the evil melts and hope is almost mandatory.
Did you save us all or merely raise the bar?

You cannot be my hero anymore. I think
I will miss you. I cannot imagine the cost
of making nice with the entitled predator
like that. I cannot imagine the cost
of not making nice when the cold
sword is already drawn.

The Bible

Before I left the cathedral
after a friend's funeral, I turned
around once more and saw
the Monsignor tenderly kissing
his bible. My heart responded
to the tenderness with longing
to be devoted like that. But

the concept of original sin
cost its original sponsor
eighty Nubian steeds payable
to the Pope then in session, and
now we all still pay off interest.

In this culture of kissing bibles,
beating women, and possessions
overly important, I still yearn
to dance with God, but I am old now.
Chances are even God would let me
sit at the edge of the dance floor
unwanted.

       I watch the dance
of devotion from my amazed
distance, always wondering
what that kiss felt like
in the celibate Monsignor's soul.

Silence

On the bus to Hermit's Rest, my forehead
pressed into the window, I watched the light
foreshadowing the sun. And then it rose,
brilliant. I exclaimed, "there's the sun."

Not having a companion, I addressed the world
at large, a small world, mind you. I admit
I claimed attention for being excited
by the vast beauty of the world.

The sun kept rising. It lit up the river
down below, the blushing canyon walls.

Two seats in front of me a handsome man
with Slavic features and a silent woman
beside him turned and gave me a look
of utter contempt.

The sun kept moving higher. The river
glittered green below.

It felt like a huge claw around my heart.
It wouldn't let go despite the magic
all around. I swore to be silent forever
and let all beauty be a secret
from now on between the sun and me.

It was a vow I will not keep.
Already I am asking. Why? What
have you done with my exuberance
and with my tenderness? Was it
of any use to you to take it like that?

I want to climb, indifferent like sun
and water, past unnecessary contempt.

This I have learned:
When I am alone, I am not ugly.

Joy

There is a tree
in the center of our lives
it is called joy.
If God doesn't want us
in his garden
we must seek another
God. And so I have
gone with my staff
and my hiking boots,
searching, and
promising my love.

But you must go without
possessions. That is
perhaps the hardest,
to go without
clinging to your roses,
trusting there will be more
or, if not, there is
always memory where
what you once have
had is yours forever.

The kiss, for example, tears
at the bus stop, his
lips on yours, forever
yours.

Lines for a Princess

I am a sheltered flower in the garden of atrocities.
You do not heed my gentleness. You do not like my rage.
Men stare over my head. I am invisible and furious.
I was told to beware of dragons, wolves, and so on.
Nobody let on that I had to beware of the prince.

How is it possible to be so dull in all this beauty
with so little time left to admire?

I am a mountain juniper, holding on to the world
in a fierce wind. There is no market for my tenderness.
I want to open the curtains of morning.
The love you never felt for me? It was so beautiful.

I am of this earth and my sequins do not hurt anyone.
I wish God would believe in me.
Don't take my legs away, then offer me stilts
and invite me to the race.

I am unhappy because I am not wanted.
I am not wanted because I am unhappy.

Perhaps I am simply one of the seeds
that never quite took, eaten by some hungry bird.
I hear the tap tap of a lonely wind on my bones.
I am not lost, just tired of the road, like an angel
with infected wings. Days whisper by. You have to
listen carefully to hear them.

We're finally enough, this earth and I, although
my yearning feels exceptionally wild today.

Beauty doesn't seem to help. I still have sparkles
on my skin from last night's dance, but now it's back
to the usual, the mash of modesty, where men choose
compromise, where they expect and are content with
dullness, and then dullness comes, as dust will settle
anywhere you do not actively defend.

I have been given this beautiful life. Sometimes I forget
to notice as I wait here, cooling toward death, a poet
who wants sequins and justice both, the wild importance
in my soul, the vertigo of colors, spice wind, and lilac rain.

I am a sheltered flower in the garden of atrocities.

The Dragon's Tale

Yes, I took the princess away.
She's hidden up in the mountains.
She's hidden from your strange
world of corsets and obedience
among the yellow flowers.
She's hidden from your male
fantasies among my cousins,
the lithe lizards. She's hidden
from your benevolent contempt
in the moss of morning dew.
You thought I was going to eat her?

ABOUT THE AUTHOR

Beate Sigriddaughter, www.sigriddaughter.net, was poet laureate of Silver City, NM (Land of Enchantment) from 2017–2019. She grew up in Nürnberg, Germany, where she began her trajectory of enchantment a five-minute walk from the castle. Alternate playgrounds, even closer to home, were World War II bomb ruins. Contrasts in her life became the norm. Her writing has received multiple Pushcart Prize nominations and a handful of poetry prizes. Keenly interested in women and their situation in the world, she created the blog *Writing In A Woman's Voice* where she publishes other women's work.

www.ingramcontent.com/pod-product-compliance
Lightning Source LLC
Chambersburg PA
CBHW020954030426
42339CB00004B/96